A Guide to Writing Chemical Formulae for Middle and High School Learners

Lisa McCulloch

Copyright © 2021 Lisa McCulloch
All rights reserved.
ISBN: 9798538694105

This guide to writing Chemical Formulae is intended to be used by middle and high school pupils who are studying Chemistry. In it you will find a thorough introduction to chemical symbols and chemical formulae along with instructions on how to work out chemical formulae using a number of different methods.

There are over 150 practise questions which will enable you to hone your technique, along with worked answers for every question to allow you to check your progress.

Everything that you need to succeed with writing chemical formulae is included in this book. A Periodic Table can be found on page 5 which you can use to look up the chemical symbols for all of the elements.

Please note, different courses in different countries vary in the exact requirements for working out chemical formulae. Always check the course specification for your course or ask a Chemistry teacher if you are unsure on which types of formula you need to know how to do.

Contents Page

The Periodic Table .... page 5

Chemical Symbols .... page 6

Chemical Formulae .... page 8

Exercise 1 – Practise writing chemical formulae .... page 10

Writing Chemical Formulae .... page 11

Writing Formulae for Compounds Made from Two Elements ...... page 13

Method 1: Valency Crossover .... page 14

Exercise 2 – Practise with valency crossover .... page 16

Method 2: Valency Crossover Using Roman Numerals .... page 20

Exercise 3 – Practise with valency crossover and roman numerals .. page 22

Method 3: Prefix Method .... page 26

Exercise 4 – Practise with prefixes .... page 28

Writing Formulae for Compounds Made from Three Elements ... page 31

Method 4: Valency Crossover with Polyatomic Ions .... page 33

Exercise 5 - Practise with polyatomic ions .... page 35

Method 5: Valency Crossover with Polyatomic Ions and Roman Numerals .... page 39

Exercise 6 - Practise with polyatomic ions and roman numerals ..... page 40

Writing Ionic Formulae .... page 44

Exercise 7 - Practise writing ionic formulae .... page 47

Answers to exercise 1 .... page 52

Answers to exercise 2 .... page 53

Answers to exercise 3 .... page 57

Answers to exercise 4 .... page 61

Answers to exercise 5 .... page 64

Answers to exercise 6 .... page 68

Answers to exercise 7 .... page 72

Group 1	Group 2											Group 3	Group 4	Group 5	Group 6	Group 7	Group 0
H Hydrogen																	He Helium
Li Lithium	Be Beryllium											B Boron	C Carbon	N Nitrogen	O Oxygen	F Fluorine	Ne Neon
Na Sodium	Mg Magnesium											Al Aluminium	Si Silicon	P Phosphorous	S Sulfur	Cl Chlorine	Ar Argon
K Potassium	Ca Calcium	Sc Scandium	Ti Titanium	V Vanadium	Cr Chromium	Mn Manganese	Fe Iron	Co Cobalt	Ni Nickel	Cu Copper	Zn Zinc	Ga Gallium	Ge Germanium	As Arsenic	Se Selenium	Br Bromine	Kr Krypton
Rb Rubidium	Sr Strontium	Y Yttrium	Zr Zirconium	Nb Niobium	Mo Molybdenum	Tc Technetium	Ru Ruthenium	Rh Rhodium	Pd Palladium	Ag Silver	Cd Cadmium	In Indium	Sn Tin	Sb Antimony	Te Tellurium	I Iodine	Xe Xenon
Cs Caesium	Ba Barium	▲	Hf Hafnium	Ta Tantalum	W Tungsten	Re Rhenium	Os Osmium	Ir Iridium	Pt Platinum	Au Gold	Hg Mercury	Tl Thallium	Pb Lead	Bi Bismuth	Po Polonium	At Astatine	Rn Radon
Fr Francium	Ra Radium	■	Rf Rutherfordium	Db Dubnium	Sg Seaborgium	Bh Bohrium	Hs Hassium	Mt Meitnerium	Ds Darmstadium	Rg Roentgenium	Cn Copernicium	Nh Nihonium	Fl Flerovium	Mc Moscovium	Lv Livermorium	Ts Tennessine	Og Oganesson

Transition Metals

▲	La Lanthanum	Ce Cerium	Pr Praseodymium	Nd Neodymium	Pm Promethium	Sm Samarium	Eu Europium	Gd Gadolinium	Tb Terbium	Dy Dysprosium	Ho Holmium	Er Erbium	Tm Thulium	Yb Ytterbium	Lu Lutetium
■	Ac Actinium	Th Thorium	Pa Protactinium	U Uranium	Np Neptunium	Pu Plutonium	Am Americium	Cm Curium	Bk Berkelium	Cf Californium	Es Einsteinium	Fm Fermium	Md Mendelevium	No Nobelium	Lr Lawrencium

Chemical Symbols

When writing chemical formulae, we use chemical symbols to represent the elements that are present. Every element has its own unique chemical symbol which can be found on many Periodic Tables.

The chemical symbol for a variety of elements is listed in the table below:

Name of Element	Chemical Symbol
Carbon	C
Nitrogen	N
Oxygen	O
Potassium	K
Phosphorous	P
Sodium	Na
Cobalt	Co

It is crucial that you pay special attention to the symbols and write them carefully. When the chemical symbol for an element is just a single letter it must be written as an uppercase letter.

Always double check the letter using a Periodic Table as you might assume that the symbol for potassium would be the letter P, but it is the letter K.

When the chemical symbol for an element is two letters, the first letter must be written as an uppercase letter, followed by the second letter written as a lowercase letter.

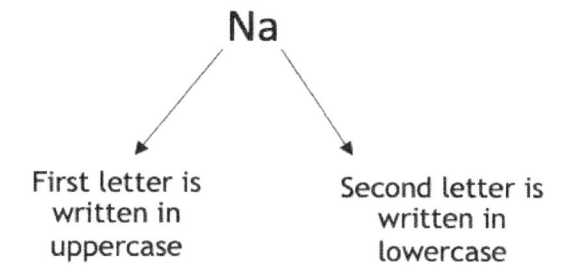

Na

First letter is written in uppercase → Second letter is written in lowercase

This is very important and is a common way in which candidates may lose marks in an exam.

The symbol for the element cobalt is Co, if the o was written as an uppercase O, the formula would read CO which represents the compound carbon monoxide, not the element cobalt!

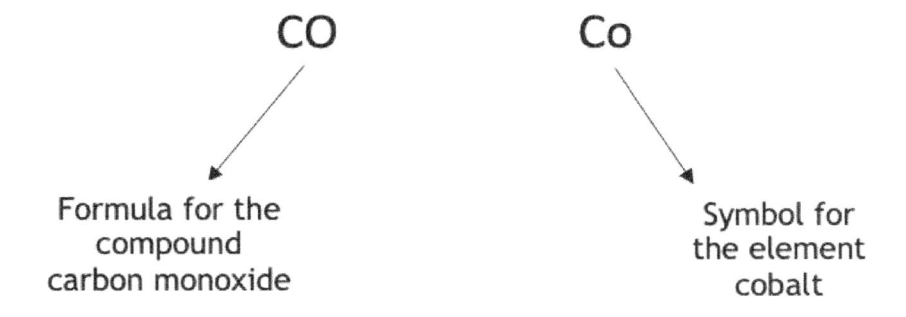

CO — Formula for the compound carbon monoxide

Co — Symbol for the element cobalt

Chemical Formulae

Chemical formulae is simply the plural of chemical formula. So rather than saying chemical formulas, we would say chemical formulae.

When writing chemical formulae, the symbols for each element present are included. The order of the symbols usually matches the order the elements appear in the name of the compound.

The chemical formula shown below represents calcium oxide

$$CaO$$

The symbol for calcium (Ca) is written before the symbol for oxide (O) because calcium is before oxide in the name of the compound.

Another way of ordering the symbols is based on the position of each element present in the Periodic Table.

The chemical formula shown below represents a substance which contains one sodium, one chlorine and one oxygen.

$$NaOCl$$

The symbol for sodium (Na) is written first as of the three elements, sodium is the furthest left on the Periodic Table. The symbol for oxygen (O) is next because as you move across the Periodic Table from left to right, we see oxygen before chlorine. The symbol for chlorine (Cl) is written last because chlorine is the furthest right on the Periodic Table.

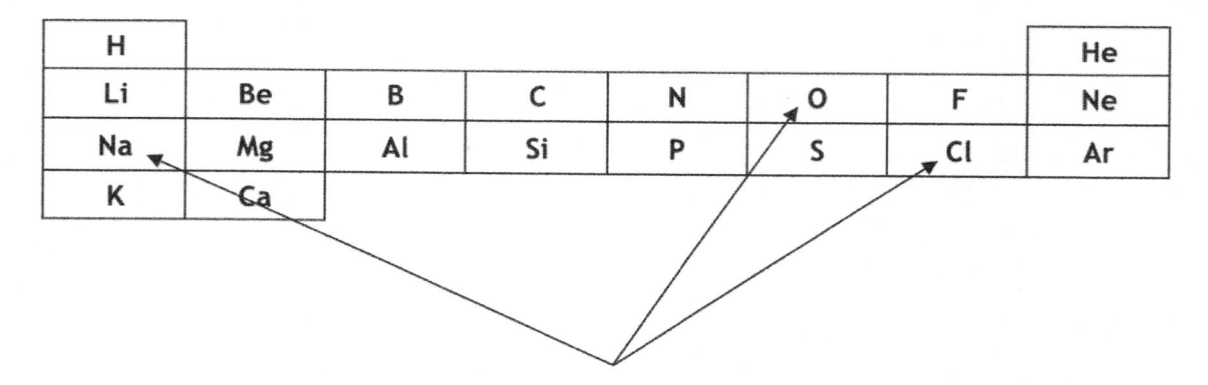

H							He
Li	Be	B	C	N	O	F	Ne
Na	Mg	Al	Si	P	S	Cl	Ar
K	Ca						

Reading from left to right the sodium (Na) is first, then oxygen (O) and then chlorine (Cl). This gives us the order the symbols should appear in the chemical formula.

Most exam boards will not penalise you for writing the symbols in a different order and some compounds don't follow these rules!

What Do the Numbers in Chemical Formulae Mean?

We use numbers in chemical formulae when there is more than one particle of an element. These numbers are always written on the bottom right of the chemical symbol.

The chemical formula shown below represents sodium carbonate.

$$Na_2CO_3$$

As you can see there are three uppercase letters, which tells use there are three elements present. Na is the symbol for the element sodium, C is the symbol for the element carbon and O is the symbol for the element oxygen.

The number 2 written on the bottom right of the Na tells us there are two sodium particles, the number 3 written on the bottom right of the O tells us there are three oxygen particles. There is no number written on the bottom right of the C which tells us there is only one carbon particle.

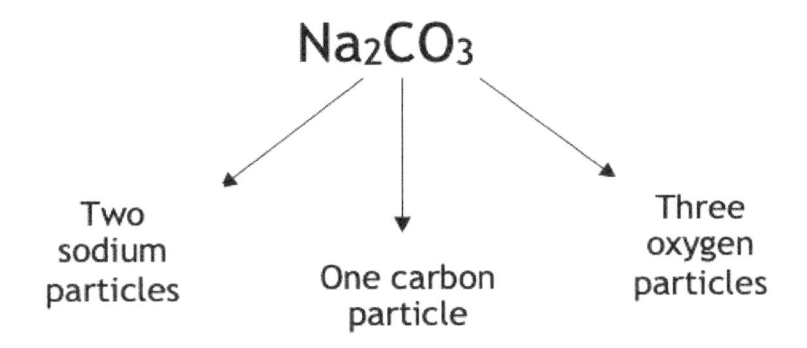

$$Na_2CO_3$$

Two sodium particles

One carbon particle

Three oxygen particles

The chemical formula of a **molecule** shows the number of **atoms** of each element present in every molecule.

For example, the chemical formula for carbon hydride is CH_4. This tells us that there are four hydrogen atoms bonded to one carbon atom.

In ionic compounds and covalent networks, the chemical formula gives the simplest ratio of atoms or ions present.

For example;
the formula for silicon oxide is SiO_2. This tells us that for every silicon atom there are two oxygen atoms.

the formula for aluminium sulfide is Al_2S_3. This tells us that for every two aluminium ions there are three sulfide ions.

When writing numbers in chemical formulae they should be less than half the size of the uppercase letter.

Exercise 1 – Practise writing chemical formulae when given the number of particles present.

Question Number	Particles Present in the Compound	Chemical Formula of the Compound
1	one magnesium and one sulfur	
2	one oxygen and two hydrogens	
3	two fluorines and one cobalt	
4	three oxygens and two aluminiums	
5	three sodium and one nitrogen	
6	one carbon, one calcium and three oxygens	
7	three oxygens, one potassium and one nitrogen	
8	one sulfur, two lithiums and four oxygens	
9	one beryllium, one carbon and three oxygens	
10	four oxygens, one sulfur and two hydrogens	
11	one aluminium, four oxygens and one phosphorous	
12	two sodium, three oxygens and one sulfur	
13	two chromiums, seven oxygens and two potassiums	

Check your answers on **page 52**. Pay special attention to uppercase and lowercase letters as well as the position of the numbers.

Writing Chemical Formulae

It is unlikely that you will be given the number of particles present in the chemical formulae, so you will need to work out the chemical formula.

The method used for working out the chemical formulae depends on a couple of factors. The first thing we must consider is how many elements does the compound contain as the method used is slightly different for compounds which contain two elements versus compounds which contain three or more elements.

How to tell if a compound is made from only two elements

The easiest way to tell if a compound is made from only two elements is to look at the name of the compound.

Compounds which end in **-ide** usually contain only two elements.

For example,

    sodium chlor**ide** is made from the elements sodium and chlorine.

    magnesium nit**ride** is made from the elements magnesium and nitrogen

    silicon ox**ide** is made from the elements silicon and oxygen

However, there are two main exceptions to this rule.

Ammonium compounds, **hydroxide** compounds and **cyanide** compounds which end in **-ide** contain more than two elements.

For example,

    Ammonium chloride is made from three elements

    Ammonium oxide is made from three elements

    Calcium **hydroxide** is made from three elements

    Aluminium **hydroxide** is made from three elements

    Sodium **cyanide** is made from three elements

    Potassium **cyanide** is made from three elements

We will look at ammonium compounds, hydroxide compounds and cyanide compounds in more detail a little later.

How to tell if a compound is made from three or more elements

The easiest way to tell if a compound is made from three or more elements is to look at the name of the compound.

Compounds which end in **-ite** or **-ate** contain three or more elements, **one of which is always oxygen**.

For example,

      calcium carbon**ate** is made from the elements calcium, carbon and oxygen

      lithium chrom**ate** is made from the elements lithium, chromium and oxygen

      iron sulf**ite** is made from the elements iron, sulfur and oxygen

Ammonium compounds and **hydroxide** compounds will also contain three or more elements.

Writing Formulae for Compounds Made from Two Elements

The chemical formula for a compound which contains only two elements can be worked out using one of the following methods:

    Method 1: **Valency Crossover**

    Method 2: **Valency Crossover Using Roman Numerals**

    Method 3: **Prefix Method**

Valency is the combining power of an element – the valency of an element indicated how many bonds it is likely to form. Elements that are in the same group of the Periodic Table will have the same valency.

The shortened version of the Periodic Table below shows the first twenty elements in the Periodic Table. Many Periodic Tables will indicate the group (or column) number.

Group 1	Group 2	Group 3	Group 4	Group 5	Group 6	Group 7	Group 0

H							He
Li	Be	B	C	N	O	F	Ne
Na	Mg	Al	Si	P	S	Cl	Ar
K	Ca						

From the Periodic Table above, we can see that hydrogen (H), lithium (Li), sodium (Na) and potassium are all in group 1 of the Periodic Table so they will all have the same valency.

Note: some Periodic Tables will refer to group 0 as group 8.

The table below indicates the valency for each group in the Periodic Table.

Group	1	2	3	4	5	6	7	0
Valency	1	2	3	4	3	2	1	0

The elements in group 0 of the Periodic Table do not usually form bonds, so they are given a valency of 0.

Method 1: Valency Crossover

The valency crossover method uses the S.V.S.D.F system.

    S - Symbols. Use a Periodic Table to find the symbols of the elements in the compound and write them down.

    V - Valency. Underneath each symbol, write the valency of the element. Use the valency table to help you with this stage until you have memorised them.

    S - Swap. Swap the valencies over.

    D - Divide (if possible). If the valencies can both be divided by the same number to give two smaller, whole numbers then do so.

    F - Formula. Write the chemical formula.

The four examples below will show you how to use this method to work out the chemical formula of a compound.

Example 1: What is the chemical formula for magnesium chloride

S	Mg	Cl	The symbols for magnesium and chlorine are found in the Periodic Table
V	2	1	Always check the valencies using the valency table!
S	1	2	The valencies have been swapped over.
D	1	2	We cannot divide the numbers 1 and 2 by the same number and keep them both whole.
F	MgCl₂		Our working tells us there is one magnesium and two chlorines

Example 2: What is the chemical formula for calcium oxide

S	Ca	O	The symbols for calcium and oxygen are found in the Periodic Table
V	2	2	Always check the valencies using the valency table!
S	2	2	The valencies have been swapped over.
D	1	1	We can divide both valencies by two to given one.
F	CaO		Our working tells us there is one calcium and one oxygen.

Example 3: What is the chemical formula for carbon sulfide

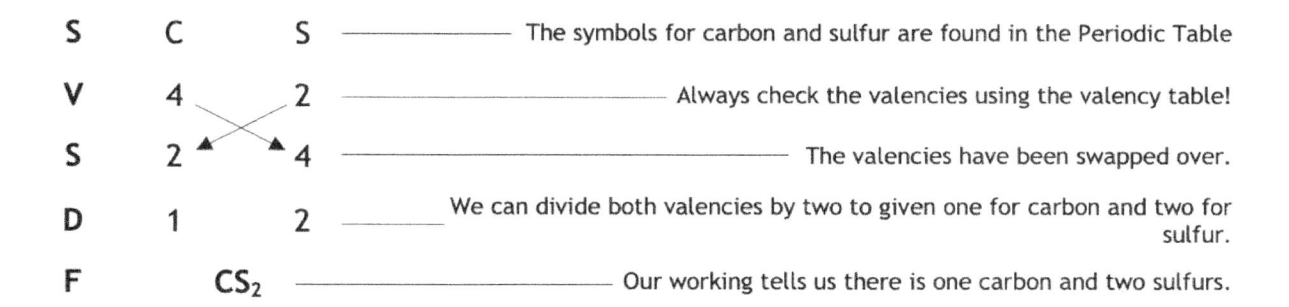

S	C	S	— The symbols for carbon and sulfur are found in the Periodic Table
V	4 ⤫ 2	— Always check the valencies using the valency table!
S	2 ⤢ 4	— The valencies have been swapped over.
D	1 2	— We can divide both valencies by two to given one for carbon and two for sulfur.
F	CS₂	— Our working tells us there is one carbon and two sulfurs.

Example 4: What is the chemical formula for aluminium oxide

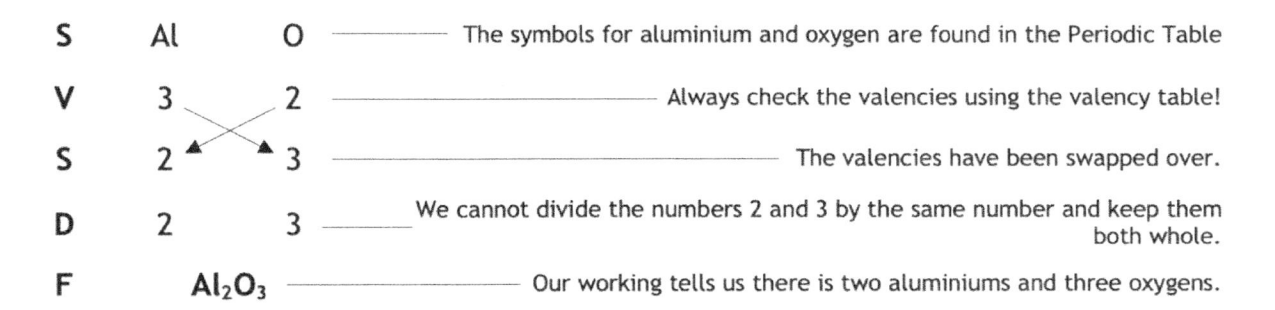

S	Al	O	— The symbols for aluminium and oxygen are found in the Periodic Table
V	3 ⤫ 2	— Always check the valencies using the valency table!
S	2 ⤢ 3	— The valencies have been swapped over.
D	2 3	— We cannot divide the numbers 2 and 3 by the same number and keep them both whole.
F	Al₂O₃	— Our working tells us there is two aluminiums and three oxygens.

You can now practise using the valency crossover method by completing **exercise 2**.

Exercise 2 – Practise writing chemical formulae using the valency crossover method.

Sodium fluoride

S

V

S

D

F

Lithium oxide

S

V

S

D

F

Phosphorous bromide

S

V

S

D

F

Hydrogen chloride

S

V

S

D

F

Caesium iodide

S

V

S

D

F

Silicon oxide

S

V

S

D

F

Sodium oxide

S

V

S

D

F

Hydrogen fluoride

S

V

S

D

F

Carbon bromide

S

V

S

D

F

Aluminium phosphide

S

V

S

D

F

Nitrogen iodide

S

V

S

D

F

Silicon nitride

S

V

S

D

F

Magnesium oxide

S

V

S

D

F

Potassium sulfide

S

V

S

D

F

Sodium hydride

S

V

S

D

F

Strontium chloride

S

V

S

D

F

Hydrogen oxide

S

V

S

D

F

Beryllium bromide

S

V

S

D

F

Boron fluoride	Aluminium chloride
S	S
V	V
S	S
D	D
F	F

Calcium phosphide	Sodium bromide
S	S
V	V
S	S
D	D
F	F

Magnesium iodide	Beryllium oxide
S	S
V	V
S	S
D	D
F	F

Check your answers on **page 53**. Pay special attention to uppercase and lowercase letters as well as the position of the numbers.

Method 2: Valency Crossover Using Roman Numerals

If you look at the Periodic Table on page 5 you will see that there is a large block of elements in between group 2 and group 3 that do not have a specific group number. This block of elements is known as the Transition Metals.

This means that the Transition metals do not have a set valency, in fact their valency can change depend on the compound they are in.

Scientists use a roman numeral in brackets after the name of the transition metal which tells us the valency of the transition metal in that compound.

Silver(II) oxide

This is the roman numeral for 2 and tells us that the valency of silver in this compound is 2.

Commonly used roman numerals in Chemistry are shown in the table below:

Roman Numeral	Meaning
I	1
II	2
III	3
IV	4
V	5
VI	6
VII	7

We can then use the S. V. S. D. F. system with the information from the roman numeral to work out the formula for compounds which contain transition metals.

Example 1: What is the chemical formula for silver(II) oxide

S	Ag	O	The symbols for silver and oxygen are found in the Periodic Table
V	2	2	The roman numeral (II) tells us the valency of silver is 2. Oxygen is in group 6 of the Periodic Table, so its valency is always 2.
S	2	2	The valencies have been swapped over.
D	1	1	We can divide both valencies by two to given one.
F	AgO		Our working tells us there is one silver and one oxygen.

Example 2: What is the chemical formula for silver(I) oxide

S	Ag	O	The symbols for silver and oxygen are found in the Periodic Table
V	1	2	The roman numeral (I) tells us the valency of silver is 1. Oxygen is in group 6 of the Periodic Table, so its valency is always 2.
S	2	1	The valencies have been swapped over.
D	2	1	We cannot divide the numbers 2 and 1 by the same number and keep them both whole.
F	Ag$_2$O		Our working tells us there is two silvers and one oxygen.

Example 3: What is the chemical formula for iron(III) chloride

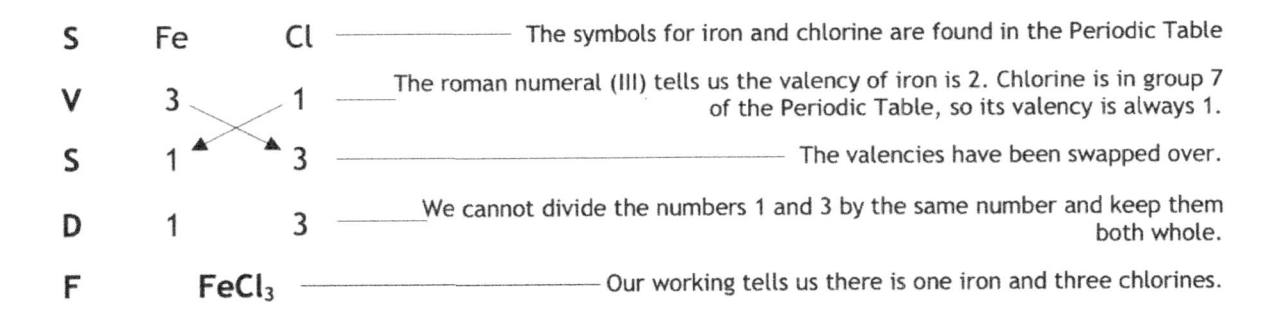

S	Fe	Cl	The symbols for iron and chlorine are found in the Periodic Table
V	3	1	The roman numeral (III) tells us the valency of iron is 2. Chlorine is in group 7 of the Periodic Table, so its valency is always 1.
S	1	3	The valencies have been swapped over.
D	1	3	We cannot divide the numbers 1 and 3 by the same number and keep them both whole.
F	FeCl$_3$		Our working tells us there is one iron and three chlorines.

You can now practise using the roman numerals with the valency crossover method by completing **exercise 3**.

Exercise 3 – Practise writing chemical formulae using roman numerals with the valency crossover method.

Copper(I) fluoride

S

V

S

D

F

Iron(III) oxide

S

V

S

D

F

Chromium(III) chloride

S

V

S

D

F

Nickel(II) fluoride

S

V

S

D

F

Titanium(IV) iodide

S

V

S

D

F

Manganese(III) sulfide

S

V

S

D

F

Vanadium(V) oxide

S

V

S

D

F

Iron(II) sulfide

S

V

S

D

F

Cadmium(II) chloride

S

V

S

D

F

Cobalt(II) bromide

S

V

S

D

F

Copper(II) oxide

S

V

S

D

F

Chromium(III) phosphide

S

V

S

D

F

Cobalt(III) oxide

S

V

S

D

F

Vanadium(IV) chloride

S

V

S

D

F

Chromium(VI) oxide

S

V

S

D

F

Iron(III) sulfide

S

V

S

D

F

Titanium(III) fluoride

S

V

S

D

F

Palladium(II) iodide

S

V

S

D

F

Mercury(II) oxide

S

V

S

D

F

Zinc(II) chloride

S

V

S

D

F

Osmium(IV) bromide

S

V

S

D

F

Chromium(VI) fluoride

S

V

S

D

F

Ruthenium(III) nitride

S

V

S

D

F

Copper(I) oxide

S

V

S

D

F

Check your answers on **page 57**. Pay special attention to uppercase and lowercase letters as well as the position of the numbers.

Method 3: Prefix Method

Sometimes, elements don't behave in the way that we expect them to. This results in the element making an unusual number of bonds which does not match the valency of the element.

Scientists came up with a special method for working out the formula for these unusual cases.

When the element in a compound makes an unusual number of bonds, the name of that compound will contain a prefix which allows us to work out the chemical formula for these compounds.

A prefix is a word that is put at the beginning of the element's name in the compound and is directly related to the number of particles of that element are present.

Commonly used prefixes in Chemistry are shown in the table:

Prefix	Meaning of Prefix
Mono	1
Di	2
Tri	3
Tetra	4
Penta	5
Hexa	6

We can use these prefixes with the **S. P. F. system** to work out the formula

S - Symbols. Use a Periodic Table to find the symbols of the elements in the compound and write them down.

P - Prefix. Underneath each symbol, write the meaning of the prefix. If there is no prefix attached to the element, write the number 1.

F - Formula. Write the chemical formula.

If there is a prefix in the formula, the prefix method must be used, attempting to use the valency crossover method will result in an incorrect answer.

Example 1: What is the chemical formula for dinitrogen tetraoxide

S	N	O	— The symbols for nitrogen and oxygen are found in the Periodic Table
P	2	4	— The prefix di means two and the prefix tetra means four. These numbers are written under the symbols.
F	N_2O_4		— Our working tells us there is two nitrogens and four oxygens.

Example 2: What is the chemical formula for carbon monoxide

S	C	O	— The symbols for carbon and oxygen are found in the Periodic Table
P	1	1	— There is no prefix attached to the carbon, so we write 1 under the carbon. The prefix mono means one, so we write 1 under the oxygen.
F	CO		— Our working tells us there is one carbon and one oxygen.

Example 3: What is the chemical formula for uranium hexafluoride

S	U	F	— The symbols for uranium and fluorine are found in the Periodic Table
P	1	6	— There is no prefix attached to the uranium, so we write 1 under the uranium. The prefix hexa means six so we write 6 under the fluorine.
F	UF_6		— Our working tells us there is one uranium and six fluorines.

Example 4: What is the chemical formula for osmium triiodide

S	Os	I	— The symbols for osmium and iodine are found in the Periodic Table
P	1	3	— There is no prefix attached to the osmium, so we write 1 under the osmium. The prefix tri means three, so we write 3 under the iodine.
F	OsI_3		— Our working tells us there is one osmium and three iodines.

You can now practise using the prefix method by completing **exercise 4**.

Exercise 4 – Practise writing chemical formulae using the prefix method

Phosphorous pentachloride

S

P

F

Carbon trioxide

S

P

F

Sulfur dioxide

S

P

F

Sulfur hexafluoride

S

P

F

Antimony tribromide

S

P

F

Diboron hexahydride

S

P

F

Xenon tetrafluoride

S

P

F

Nitrogen dioxide

S

P

F

Carbon disulfide

S

P

F

Disilicon hexabromide

S

P

F

Dihydrogen dioxide

S

P

F

Dinitrogen trioxide

S

P

F

Selenium trioxide

S

P

F

Diphosphorous tetrafluroide

S

P

F

Iodine pentafluoride

S

P

F

Dichlorine monoxide

S

P

F

Oxygen dibromide

S

P

F

Sulfur triflouride

S

P

F

Boron monofluoride

S

P

F

Tetraphosphorous trisulfide

S

P

F

Tetraphosphorous pentasulfide

S

P

F

Dinitrogen monoxide

S

P

F

Diphosphorous pentaoxide

S

P

F

Diselenium dichloride

S

P

F

Check your answers on **page 61**. Pay special attention to uppercase and lowercase letters as well as the position of the numbers.

Writing Formulae for Compounds Made from Three or More Elements

The chemical formula for a compound which contain three or more elements can be worked out using one of the following methods:

Method 4: **Valency Crossover with Polyatomic Ions**

Method 5: **Valency Crossover with Roman Numerals and Polyatomic Ions**

Polyatomic Ions

Polyatomic ions contain two or more atoms bonded together. They can be positively or negatively charged.

The sulfate group ion is represented as:

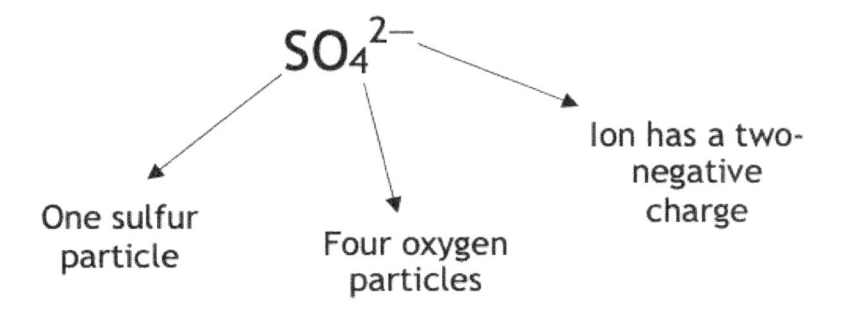

$$SO_4^{2-}$$

- One sulfur particle
- Four oxygen particles
- Ion has a two-negative charge

The hydroxide ion is represented as:

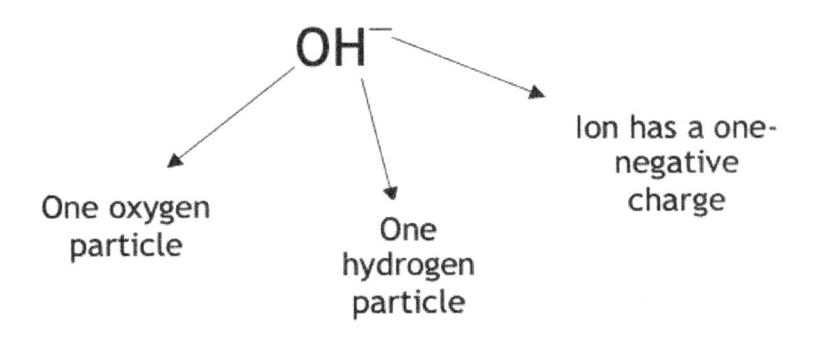

$$OH^-$$

- One oxygen particle
- One hydrogen particle
- Ion has a one-negative charge

Polyatomic ions stick together during chemical reactions so can be treated as if they are one species when working out chemical formula.

For exams, a list of polyatomic ions will usually be provided on a Data Sheet or in a Data Book.

Some common polyatomic ions are listed in the table below. Keep referring to this table as needed.

Name of Polyatomic Ion	Formula of Polyatomic Ion	Valency of Polyatomic Ion
Ammonium	NH_4^+	1
Hydroxide	OH^-	1
Cyanide	CN^-	1
Nitrite	NO_2^-	1
Nitrate	NO_3^-	1
Hydrogen sulfate	HSO_4^-	1
Hydrogen carbonate	HCO_3^-	1
Hypochlorite	ClO^-	1
Permanganate	MnO_4^-	1
Sulfite	SO_3^{2-}	2
Sulfate	SO_4^{2-}	2
Carbonate	CO_3^{2-}	2
Dichromate	$Cr_2O_7^{2-}$	2
Chromate	CrO_4^{2-}	2
Phosphate	PO_4^{3-}	3

As you can see, the valency of the polyatomic ion is the same as the power of the charge. So, if a polyatomic ion has a charge of 2+, it will have a valency of 2. If it has a charge of —, it will have a valency of 1.

Note: polyatomic ions with a charge of one plus or one minus would be written as + or —, rather than 1+ or 1—.

Method 4: Valency Crossover with Polyatomic Ions

We can use the formula for a polyatomic ion with the S. V. S. D. F. method to work out the chemical formula for compounds which contain polyatomic ions.

An important point to note is that if there is more than one polyatomic ion, it must be placed inside a bracket, with the number of those ions written on the outside of the backet.

To see this more clearly, let's look at magnesium nitrate:

S	Mg	NO$_3$	The symbol for magnesium is found in the Periodic Table. The formula for the nitrate ion is found from the polyatomic ion table.
V	2	1	Magnesium is in group 2, so its valency is 2. The nitrate ion has a one-negative charge, so its valency is 1.
S	1	2	The valencies have been swapped over.
D	1	2	We cannot divide the numbers 1 and 2 by the same number and keep them both whole.
F	Mg(NO$_3$)$_2$		Our working tells us there is one magnesium and two nitrates.

Let's look at the formula for magnesium nitrate with and without the bracket around the nitrate:

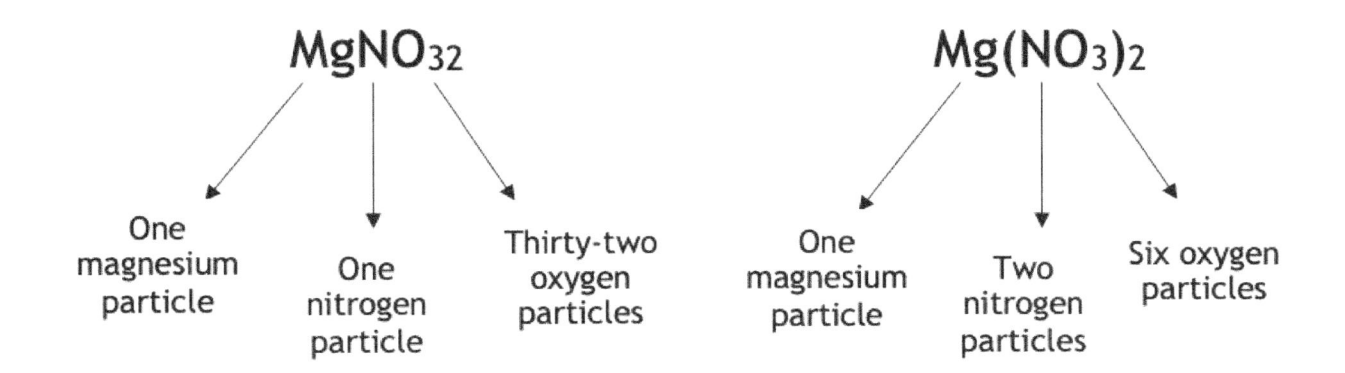

MgNO$_{32}$
- One magnesium particle
- One nitrogen particle
- Thirty-two oxygen particles

Mg(NO$_3$)$_2$
- One magnesium particle
- Two nitrogen particles
- Six oxygen particles

Without the bracket around the nitrate the formula is very different. The formula on the left is incorrect.

Example 1: What is the chemical formula for sodium carbonate

S	Na	CO₃	— The symbol for sodium is found in the Periodic Table. The formula for carbonate is found in the polyatomic ion table.
V	1	2	— Sodium is in group 1, so its valency is always 1. Carbonate has a 2- charge so its valency is 2.
S	2	1	— The valencies have been swapped over.
D	2	1	— We cannot divide the numbers 2 and 1 by the same number and keep them both whole.
F	Na₂CO₃		— Our working tells us there is two sodiums and one carbonate.

Example 2: What is the chemical formula for aluminium phosphate

S	Al	PO₄	— The symbol for aluminium is found in the Periodic Table. The formula for phosphate is found in the polyatomic ion table.
V	3	3	— Aluminium is in group 3, so its valency is always 3. Phosphate has a 3- charge so its valency is 3.
S	3	3	— The valencies have been swapped over.
D	1	1	— We can divide both valencies by three to give one.
F	AlPO₄		— Our working tells us there is one aluminium and one phosphate.

Example 3: What is the chemical formula for ammonium sulfate

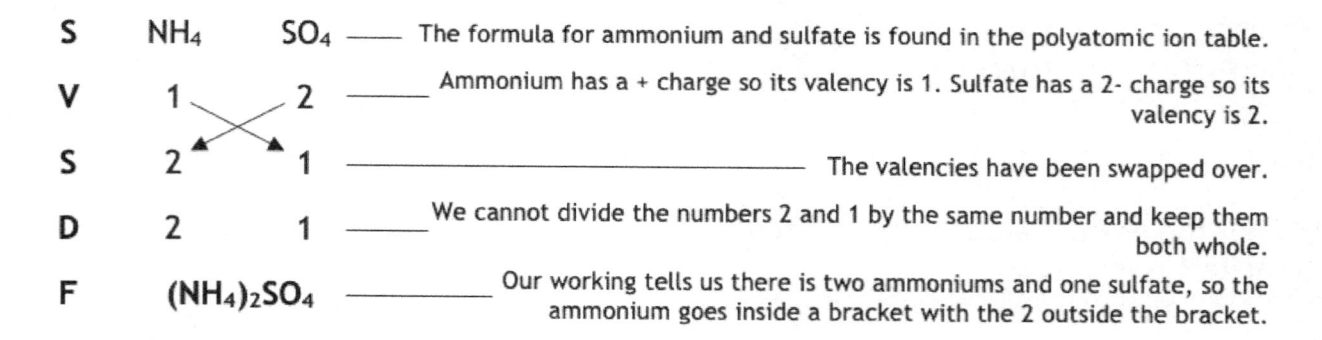

S	NH₄	SO₄	— The formula for ammonium and sulfate is found in the polyatomic ion table.
V	1	2	— Ammonium has a + charge so its valency is 1. Sulfate has a 2- charge so its valency is 2.
S	2	1	— The valencies have been swapped over.
D	2	1	— We cannot divide the numbers 2 and 1 by the same number and keep them both whole.
F	(NH₄)₂SO₄		— Our working tells us there is two ammoniums and one sulfate, so the ammonium goes inside a bracket with the 2 outside the bracket.

You can now practise writing chemical formulae with polyatomic ions by completing **exercise 5**.

Exercise 5 - Practise writing chemical formulae using polyatomic ions

Ammonium chloride

S

V

S

D

F

Potassium phosphate

S

V

S

D

F

Calcium sulfite

S

V

S

D

F

Aluminium hydroxide

S

V

S

D

F

Lithium cyanide

S

V

S

D

F

Magnesium nitrate

S

V

S

D

F

Sodium hydrogencarbonate

S

V

S

D

F

Beryllium nitrite

S

V

S

D

F

Aluminium sulfate

S

V

S

D

F

Caesium hypochlorite

S

V

S

D

F

Potassium permanganate

S

V

S

D

F

Strontium hydrogensulfate

S

V

S

D

F

Calcium hydroxide

S

V

S

D

F

Magnesium cyanide

S

V

S

D

F

Sodium sulfate

S

V

S

D

F

Rubidium carbonate

S

V

S

D

F

Potassium dichromate

S

V

S

D

F

Ammonium nitrate

S

V

S

D

F

Potassium hydroxide

S

V

S

D

F

Sodium chromate

S

V

S

D

F

Strontium nitrite

S

V

S

D

F

Beryllium hypochlorite

S

V

S

D

F

Barium sulfite

S

V

S

D

F

Ammonium carbonate

S

V

S

D

F

Check your answers on **page 64**. Pay special attention to uppercase and lowercase letters as well as the position of the numbers.

Method 5: Valency Crossover with Roman Numerals and Polyatomic Ions

It is also possible to have compounds which contain transition metals and polyatomic ions. Remember, the valency of the transition metal is indicated by a roman numeral inside a bracket after the name of the transition metal.

We can then use the formula for a polyatomic ion and the information given by the roman numeral with the S. V. S. D. F. method to work out the chemical formula for compounds which contain transition metals and polyatomic ions.

Example 1: What is the chemical formula for iron(II) sulfate

S	Fe	SO₄	— The symbol for iron is found in the Periodic Table. The formula for sulfate is found in the polyatomic ion table.
V	2	2	— The roman numeral (II) tells use the valency of iron is 2. Sulfate has a 2- charge so its valency is 2.
S	2	2	— The valencies have been swapped over.
D	1	1	— We can divide both valencies by two to give one.
F	FeSO₄		— Our working tells us there is one iron and one sulfate.

Example 2: What is the chemical formula for chromium(III) nitrate

S	Cr	NO₃	— The symbol for chromium is found in the Periodic Table. The formula for nitrate is found in the polyatomic ion table.
V	3	1	— The roman numeral (III) tells use the valency of chromium is 3. Nitrate has a - charge so its valency is 1.
S	1	3	— The valencies have been swapped over.
D	1	3	— We cannot divide the numbers 1 and 3 by the same number and keep them both whole.
F	Cr(NO₃)₃		— Our working tells us there is one chromium and three nitrates, so the nitrate goes inside a bracket with the 3 outside the bracket.

Example 3: What is the chemical formula for nickel(I) cyanide

S	Ni	CN	— The symbol for nickel is found in the Periodic Table. The formula for cyanide is found in the polyatomic ion table.
V	1	1	— Ammonium has a + charge so its valency is 1. Sulfate has a 2- charge so its valency is 2.
S	1	1	— The valencies have been swapped over.
D	1	1	— We cannot divide the numbers 1 by the same number and keep them both whole.
F	NiCN		— Our working tells us there is one nickel and one cyanide.

You can now practise writing chemical formulae with transition metals and polyatomic ions by completing **exercise 6**.

Exercise 6 - Practise writing chemical formulae using roman numerals and polyatomic ions

Vanadium(II) sulfate

S

V

S

D

F

Vanadium(III) hydroxide

S

V

S

D

F

Titanium(II) nitrate

S

V

S

D

F

Copper(I) cyanide

S

V

S

D

F

Manganese(II) carbonate

S

V

S

D

F

Iron(III) sulfite

S

V

S

D

F

Cobalt(II) nitrite

S

V

S

D

F

Zinc(II) phosphate

S

V

S

D

F

Palladium(II) sulfate

S

V

S

D

F

Vanadium(IV) hydrogensulfate

S

V

S

D

F

Ruthenium(III) nitrate

S

V

S

D

F

Copper(II) carbonate

S

V

S

D

F

Tungsten(III) cyanide

S

V

S

D

F

Chromium(II) hypochlorite

S

V

S

D

F

Nickel(II) carbonate

S

V

S

D

F

Iron(III) phosphate

S

V

S

D

F

Cadmium(II) hydroxide

S

V

S

D

F

Niobium(V) nitrate

S

V

S

D

F

Manganese(II) carbonate

S

V

S

D

F

Silver(I) nitrate

S

V

S

D

F

Cobalt(II) hydroxide

S

V

S

D

F

Copper(I) chromate

S

V

S

D

F

Zinc(II) sulfate

S

V

S

D

F

Nickel(II) phosphate

S

V

S

D

F

Check your answers on **page 68**. Pay special attention to uppercase and lowercase letters as well as the position of the numbers.

Writing Ionic Formulae

Writing ionic formulae is very similar to the chemical formulae that we have looked at so far, with the exception that ionic formula includes the charges on each ion present in the formula.

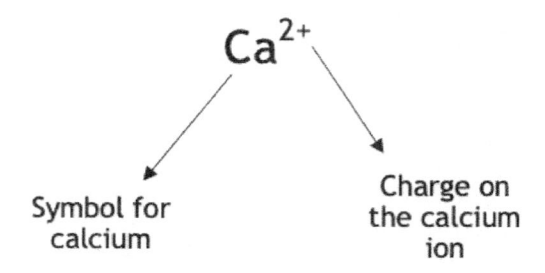

$$Ca^{2+}$$

Symbol for calcium → Ca

Charge on the calcium ion → 2+

The charge on an ion depends on what group of the Periodic Table it is found in and is closely related to that element's valency. The table shows the charge on ions for all the groups in the Periodic Table.

Group	Valency	Charge on Ion
1	1	+
2	2	2+
3	3	3+
4	4	Do not usually form ions
5	3	3−
6	2	2−
7	1	−
0	0	Do not usually form ions

The charge on a transition metal ion is also closely related to the valency on the transition metal. The table shows the charge on transition metal ions depending on their valency.

Notice that metal ions always carry a positive charge.

Roman Numeral	Valency	Charge on Ion
I	1	+
II	2	2+
III	3	3+
IV	4	4+
V	5	5+
VI	6	6+
VII	7	7+

The charge on polyatomic ions is given on the polyatomic ion table.

When there is more than one of an ion in the formula, the symbol and charge on the ion must be placed inside a bracket with the number of that ion on the outside of the bracket.

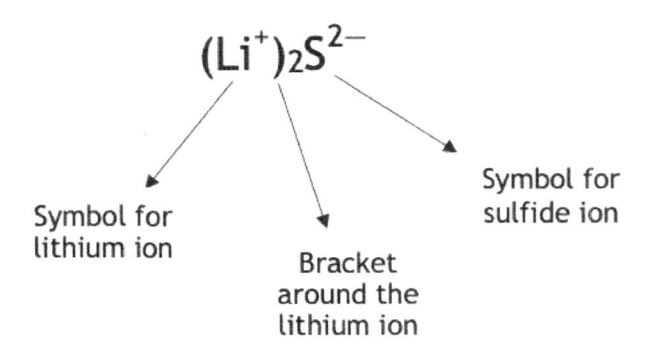

$$(Li^+)_2 S^{2-}$$

Symbol for lithium ion

Bracket around the lithium ion

Symbol for sulfide ion

Example 1: What is the ionic formula for magnesium chloride

S	Mg^{2+}	Cl^-	The symbol for magnesium and chlorine are found in the Periodic Table. The charge on each ion is found using the information in the charges on ion table.
V	2	1	Magnesium is in group 2, so it has a valency of 2. Chlorine is in group 7, so it has a valency of 1.
S	1	2	The valencies have been swapped over.
D	1	2	We cannot divide the numbers 1 and 2 by the same number and keep them both whole.
F	$Mg^{2+}(Cl^-)_2$		Our working tells us there is one magnesium and two chlorines. The symbol and charge on chlorine are placed inside a bracket.

Example 2: What is the ionic formula for iron(III) oxide

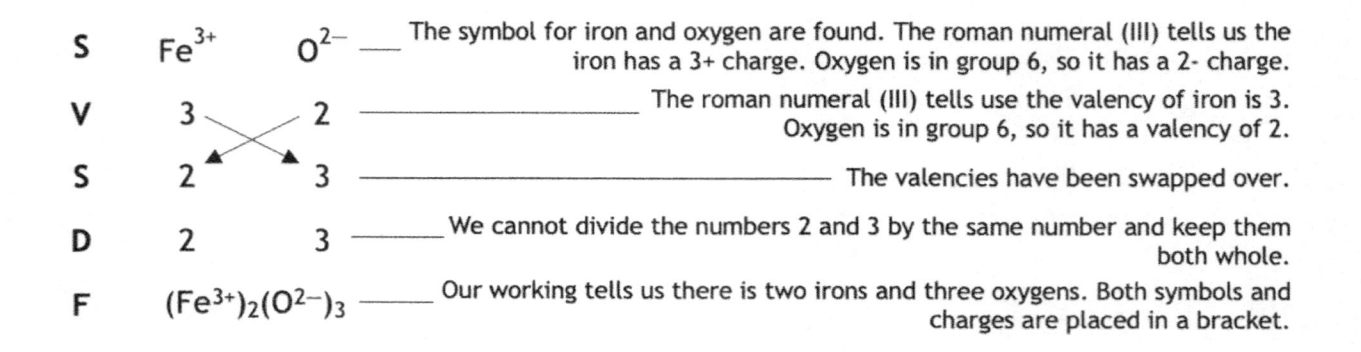

S	Fe^{3+}	O^{2-}	The symbol for iron and oxygen are found. The roman numeral (III) tells us the iron has a 3+ charge. Oxygen is in group 6, so it has a 2- charge.
V	3	2	The roman numeral (III) tells use the valency of iron is 3. Oxygen is in group 6, so it has a valency of 2.
S	2	3	The valencies have been swapped over.
D	2	3	We cannot divide the numbers 2 and 3 by the same number and keep them both whole.
F	$(Fe^{3+})_2(O^{2-})_3$		Our working tells us there is two irons and three oxygens. Both symbols and charges are placed in a bracket.

Example 3: What is the ionic formula for calcium carbonate

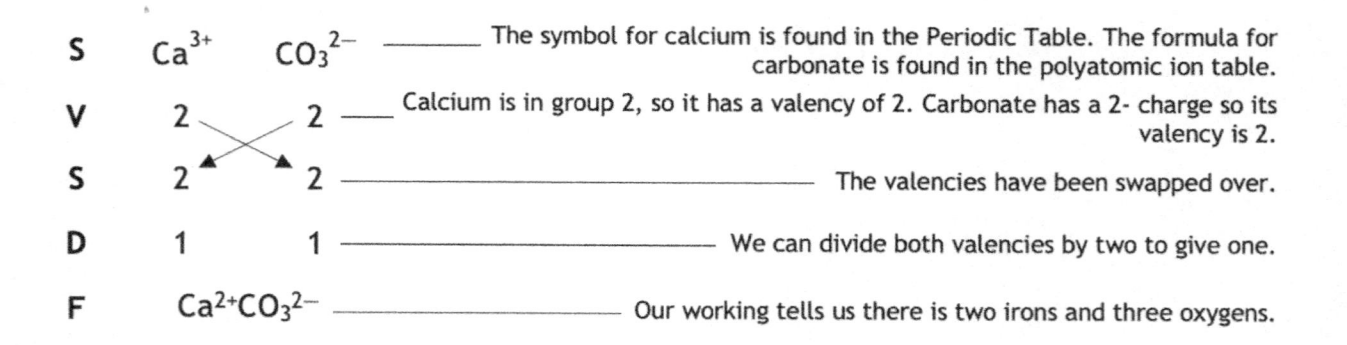

S	Ca^{3+}	CO_3^{2-}	The symbol for calcium is found in the Periodic Table. The formula for carbonate is found in the polyatomic ion table.
V	2	2	Calcium is in group 2, so it has a valency of 2. Carbonate has a 2- charge so its valency is 2.
S	2	2	The valencies have been swapped over.
D	1	1	We can divide both valencies by two to give one.
F	$Ca^{2+}CO_3^{2-}$		Our working tells us there is two irons and three oxygens.

You can now practise writing ionic formulae with polyatomic ions by completing **exercise 7**.

Exercise 7 - Practise writing ionic formulae

Sodium fluoride

S

V

S

D

F

Lithium sulfide

S

V

S

D

F

Aluminium oxide

S

V

S

D

F

Magnesium oxide

S

V

S

D

F

Copper(II) chloride

S

V

S

D

F

Potassium nitrate

S

V

S

D

F

Ammonium iodide

S

V

S

D

F

Vanadium(V) oxide

S

V

S

D

F

Nickel(II) nitrate

S

V

S

D

F

Zinc(II) sulfite

S

V

S

D

F

Potassium hydrogencarbonate

S

V

S

D

F

Lithium nitride

S

V

S

D

F

Calcium hydroxide

S

V

S

D

F

Manganese(II) chloride

S

V

S

D

F

Rubidium iodide

S

V

S

D

F

Cobalt(III) phosphate

S

V

S

D

F

Copper(II) sulfate

S

V

S

D

F

Strontium nitrite

S

V

S

D

F

Ammonium cyanide	Chromium(IV) oxide
S	S
V	V
S	S
D	D
F	F

Sodium hypochlorite	Silver(I) sulfide
S	S
V	V
S	S
D	D
F	F

Barium nitrate	Potassium permanganate
S	S
V	V
S	S
D	D
F	F

Check your answers on **page 72**. Pay special attention to uppercase and lowercase letters as well as the position of the numbers.

Answers to exercises 1 to 7

Exercise 1 — Answers

Question Number	Particles Present in the Compound	Chemical Formula of the Compound
1	one magnesium and one sulfur	MgS
2	one oxygen and two hydrogens	H_2O
3	two fluorines and one cobalt	CoF_2
4	three oxygens and two aluminiums	Al_2O_3
5	three sodium and one nitrogen	Na_3N
6	one carbon, one calcium and three oxygens	$CaCO_3$
7	three oxygens, one potassium and one nitrogen	KNO_3
8	one sulfur, two lithiums and four oxygens	Li_2SO_4
9	one beryllium, one calcium and three oxygens	$BeCO_3$
10	four oxygens, one sulfur and two hydrogens	H_2SO_4
11	one aluminium, four oxygens and one phosphorous	$AlPO_4$
12	two sodium, three oxygens and one sulfur	Na_2SO_3
13	two chromiums, seven oxygens and two potassiums	$K_2Cr_2O_7$

Exercise 2 — Answers

Sodium fluoride

S	Na	F
V	1	1
S	1	1
D	1	1
F	NaF	

Lithium oxide

S	Li	O
V	1	2
S	2	1
D	2	1
F	Li$_2$O	

Phosphorous bromide

S	P	Br
V	3	1
S	1	3
D	1	3
F	PBr$_3$	

Hydrogen chloride

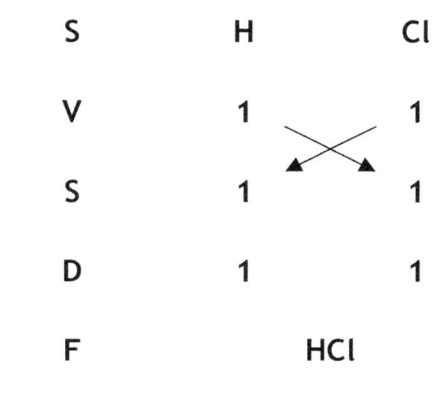

S	H	Cl
V	1	1
S	1	1
D	1	1
F	HCl	

Caesium iodide

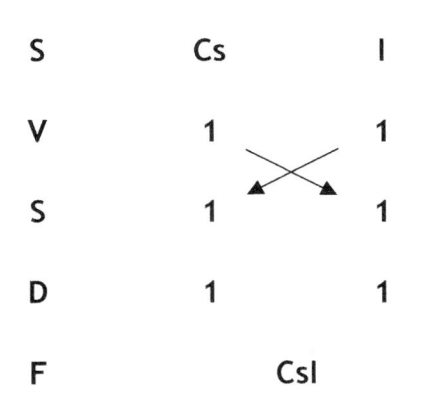

S	Cs	I
V	1	1
S	1	1
D	1	1
F	CsI	

Silicon oxide

S	Si	O
V	4	2
S	2	4
D	1	2
F	SiO$_2$	

Sodium oxide

S	Na	O
V	1	2
S	2	1
D	2	1

F Na₂O

Hydrogen fluoride

S	H	F
V	1	1
S	1	1
D	1	1

F HF

Carbon bromide

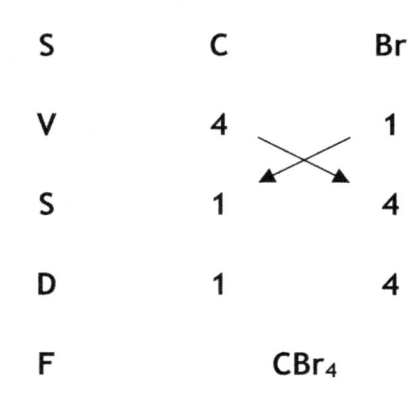

S	C	Br
V	4	1
S	1	4
D	1	4

F CBr₄

Aluminium phosphide

S	Al	P
V	3	3
S	3	3
D	1	1

F AlP

Nitrogen iodide

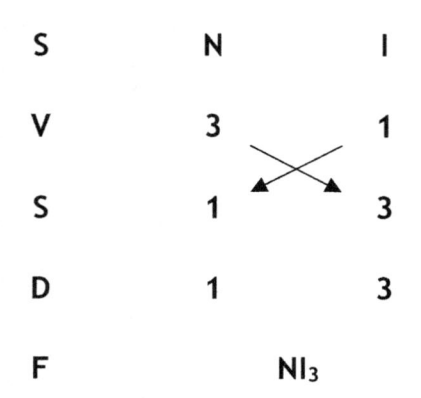

S	N	I
V	3	1
S	1	3
D	1	3

F NI₃

Silicon nitride

S	Si	N
V	4	3
S	3	4
D	3	4

F Si₃N₄

Magnesium oxide

S	Mg	O
V	2	2
S	2	2
D	1	1
F		MgO

Strontium chloride

S	Sr	Cl
V	2	1
S	1	2
D	1	2
F		SrCl$_2$

Potassium sulfide

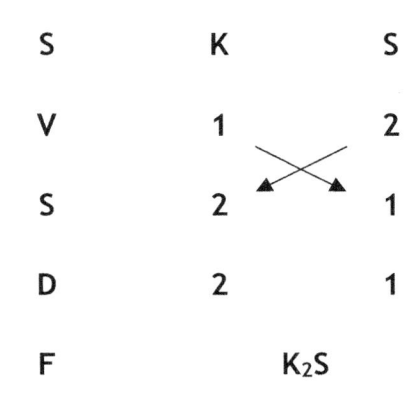

S	K	S
V	1	2
S	2	1
D	2	1
F		K$_2$S

Hydrogen oxide

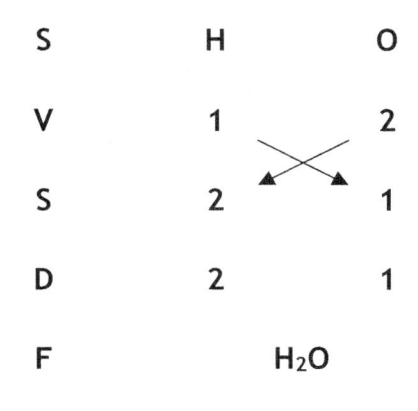

S	H	O
V	1	2
S	2	1
D	2	1
F		H$_2$O

Sodium hydride

S	Na	H
V	1	1
S	1	1
D	1	1
F		NaH

Beryllium bromide

S	Be	Br
V	2	1
S	1	2
D	1	2
F		BeBr$_2$

Boron fluoride

S	B	F
V	3	1
S	1	3
D	1	3
F		BF_3

Aluminium chloride

S	Al	Cl
V	3	1
S	1	3
D	1	3
F		$AlCl_3$

Calcium phosphide

S	Ca	P
V	2	3
S	3	2
D	3	2
F		Ca_3P_2

Sodium bromide

S	Na	Br
V	1	1
S	1	1
D	1	1
F		NaBr

Magnesium iodide

S	Mg	I
V	2	1
S	1	2
D	1	2
F		MgI_2

Beryllium oxide

S	Be	O
V	2	2
S	2	2
D	1	1
F		BeO

Exercise 3 — Answers

Copper(I) fluoride

S	Cu	F
V	1	1
S	1	1
D	1	1
F		CuF

Iron(III) oxide

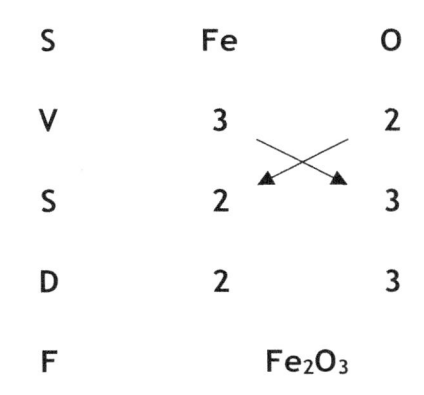

S	Fe	O
V	3	2
S	2	3
D	2	3
F		Fe_2O_3

Chromium(III) chloride

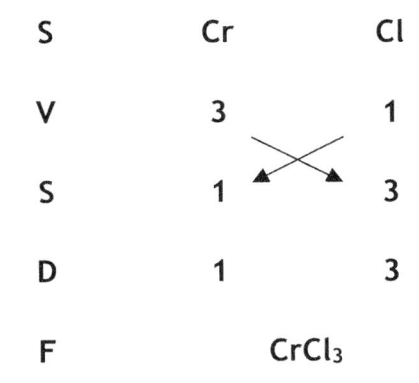

S	Cr	Cl
V	3	1
S	1	3
D	1	3
F		$CrCl_3$

Nickel(II) fluoride

S	Ni	F
V	2	1
S	1	2
D	1	2
F		NiF_2

Titanium(IV) iodide

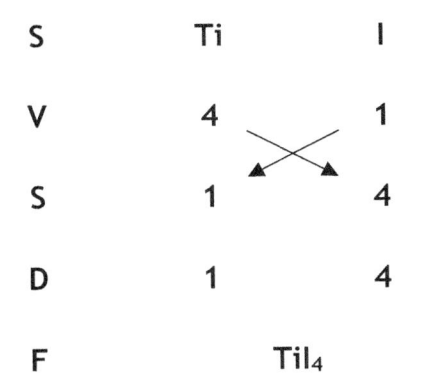

S	Ti	I
V	4	1
S	1	4
D	1	4
F		TiI_4

Manganese(III) sulfide

S	Mn	S
V	3	2
S	2	3
D	2	3
F		Mn_2S_3

Vanadium(V) oxide

S   V   O
V   5   2
S   2   5
D   2   5
F   V₂O₅

Cobalt(II) bromide

S   Co   Br
V   2   1
S   1   2
D   1   2
F   CoBr₂

Iron(II) sulfide

S   Fe   S
V   2   2
S   2   2
D   1   1
F   FeS

Copper(II) oxide

S   Cu   O
V   2   2
S   2   2
D   1   1
F   CuO

Cadmium(II) chloride

S   Cr   Cl
V   2   1
S   1   2
D   1   2
F   CrCl₂

Chromium(III) phosphide

S   Cr   P
V   3   3
S   3   3
D   1   1
F   CrP

Cobalt(III) oxide

S	Co	O
V	3	2
S	2	3
D	2	3
F	Co$_2$O$_3$	

Iron(III) sulfide

S	Fe	S
V	3	2
S	2	3
D	2	3
F	Fe$_2$S$_3$	

Vanadium(IV) chloride

S	V	Cl
V	4	1
S	1	4
D	1	4
F	VCl$_4$	

Titanium(III) fluoride

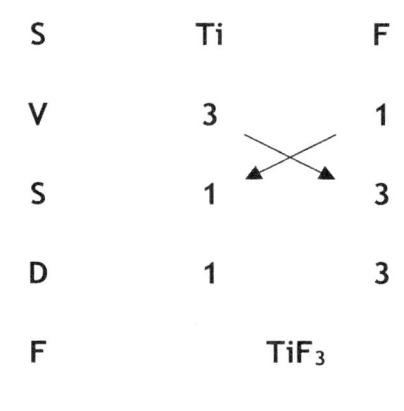

S	Ti	F
V	3	1
S	1	3
D	1	3
F	TiF$_3$	

Chromium(VI) oxide

S	Cr	O
V	6	2
S	2	6
D	1	3
F	CrO$_3$	

Palladium(II) iodide

S	Pd	I
V	2	1
S	1	2
D	1	2
F	PdI$_2$	

Mercury(II) oxide

S	Hg	O
V	2	2
S	2	2
D	1	1
F		HgO

Zinc(II) chloride

S	Zn	Cl
V	2	1
S	1	2
D	1	2
F		ZnCl$_2$

Osmium(IV) bromide

S	Os	Br
V	4	1
S	1	4
D	1	4
F		OsBr$_4$

Chromium(VI) fluoride

S	Cr	F
V	6	1
S	1	6
D	1	6
F		CrF$_6$

Ruthenium(III) nitride

S	Ru	N
V	3	3
S	3	3
D	1	1
F		RuN

Copper(I) oxide

S	Cu	O
V	1	2
S	2	1
D	2	1
F		Cu$_2$O

Exercise 4 — Answers

Phosphorous pentachloride

S	P	Cl
P	1	5
F		PCl₅

Carbon trioxide

S	C	O
P	1	3
F		CO₃

Sulfur dioxide

S	S	O
P	1	2
F		SO₂

Sulfur hexafluoride

S	S	F
P	1	6
F		SF₆

Antimony tribromide

S	Sb	Br
P	1	3
F		SbBr₃

Diboron hexahydride

S	B	H
P	2	6
F		B₂H₆

Xenon tetrafluoride

S	Xe	F
P	1	4
F		XeF₄

Nitrogen dioxide

S	N	O
P	1	2
F		NO₂

Carbon disulfide

S	C	S
P	1	2
F		CS_2

Selenium trioxide

S	Se	O
P	1	3
F		SeO_3

Disilicon hexabromide

S	Si	Br
P	2	6
F		Si_2Br_6

Diphosphorous tetrafluroide

S	P	F
P	2	4
F		P_2F_4

Dihydrogen dioxide

S	H	O
P	2	2
F		H_2O_2

Iodine pentafluoride

S	I	F
P	1	5
F		IF_5

Dinitrogen trioxide

S	N	O
P	2	3
F		N_2O_3

Dichlorine monoxide

S	Cl	O
P	2	1
F		Cl_2O

Oxygen dibromide				Tetraphosphorous pentasulfide		
S	O	Br		S	P	S
P	1	2		P	4	5
F	OBr₂			F	P₄S₅	

Sulfur triflouride				Dinitrogen monoxide		
S	S	F		S	N	O
P	1	3		P	2	1
F	SF₃			F	N₂O	

Boron monofluoride				Diphosphorous pentaoxide		
S	B	F		S	P	O
P	1	1		P	2	5
F	BF			F	P₂O₅	

Tetraphosphorous trisulfide				Diselenium dichloride		
S	P	S		S	Se	Cl
P	4	3		P	2	2
F	P₄S₃			F	Se₂Cl₂	

Exercise 5 — Answers

Ammonium chloride

S	NH₄	Cl
V	1	1
S	1	1
D	1	1
F		NH₄Cl

Potassium phosphate

S	K	PO₄
V	1	3
S	3	1
D	3	1
F		K₃PO₄

Calcium sulfite

S	Ca	SO₃
V	2	2
S	2	2
D	1	1
F		CaSO₃

Aluminium hydroxide

S	Al	OH
V	3	1
S	1	3
D	1	3
F		Al(OH)₃

Lithium cyanide

S	Li	CN
V	1	1
S	1	1
D	1	1
F		LiCN

Magnesium nitrate

S	Mg	NO₃
V	2	1
S	1	2
D	1	2
F		Mg(NO₃)₂

Sodium hydrogencarbonate

S	Na	HCO$_3$
V	1	1
S	1	1
D	1	1
F	NaHCO$_3$	

Caesium hypochlorite

S	Cs	ClO
V	1	1
S	1	1
D	1	1
F	CsClO	

Beryllium nitrite

S	Be	NO$_3$
V	2	1
S	1	2
D	1	2
F	Be(NO$_3$)$_2$	

Potassium permanganate

S	K	MnO$_4$
V	1	1
S	1	1
D	1	1
F	KMnO$_4$	

Aluminium sulfate

S	Al	SO$_4$
V	3	2
S	2	3
D	2	3
F	Al$_2$(SO$_4$)$_3$	

Strontium hydrogensulfate

S	Sr	HSO$_4$
V	2	1
S	1	2
D	1	2
F	Sr(HSO$_4$)$_2$	

Calcium hydroxide

S	Ca	OH
V	2	1
S	1	2
D	1	2
F	Ca(OH)₂	

Rubidium carbonate

S	Rb	CO₃
V	1	2
S	2	1
D	2	1
F	Rb₂CO₃	

Magnesium cyanide

S	Mg	CN
V	2	1
S	1	2
D	1	2
F	Mg(CN)₂	

Potassium dichromate

S	K	Cr₂O₇
V	1	2
S	2	1
D	2	1
F	K₂Cr₂O₇	

Sodium sulfate

S	Na	SO₄
V	1	2
S	2	1
D	2	1
F	Na₂SO₄	

Ammonium nitrate

S	NH₄	NO₃
V	1	1
S	1	1
D	1	1
F	NH₄NO₃	

Potassium hydroxide				Sodium chromate		
S	K	OH		S	Na	CrO₄
V	1	1		V	1	2
S	1	1		S	2	1
D	1	1		D	2	1
F	KOH			F	Na₂CrO₄	

Strontium nitrite				Beryllium hypochlorite		
S	Sr	NO₃		S	Be	ClO
V	2	1		V	2	1
S	1	2		S	1	2
D	1	2		D	1	2
F	Sr(NO₃)₂			F	Be(ClO)₂	

Barium sulfite				Ammonium carbonate		
S	Ba	SO₃		S	NH₄	CO₃
V	2	2		V	1	2
S	2	2		S	2	1
D	1	1		D	2	1
F	BaSO₃			F	(NH₄)₂CO₃	

Exercise 6 — Answers

Vanadium(II) sulfate

S	V	SO$_4$
V	2	2
S	2	2
D	1	1
F		VSO$_4$

Vanadium(III) hydroxide

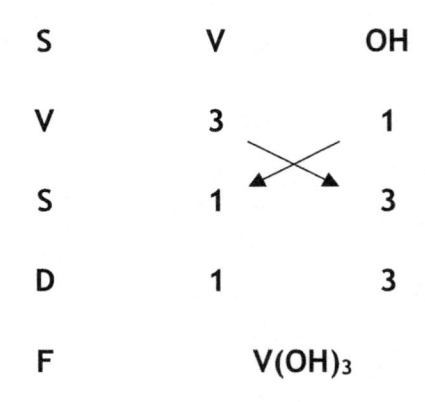

S	V	OH
V	3	1
S	1	3
D	1	3
F		V(OH)$_3$

Titanium(II) nitrate

S	Ti	NO$_3$
V	2	1
S	1	2
D	1	2
F		Ti(NO$_3$)$_2$

Copper(I) cyanide

S	Cu	CN
V	1	1
S	1	1
D	1	1
F		CuCN

Manganese(II) carbonate

S	Mn	CO$_3$
V	2	2
S	2	2
D	1	1
F		MnCO$_3$

Iron(III) sulfite

S	Fe	SO$_3$
V	3	2
S	2	3
D	2	3
F		Fe$_2$(SO$_3$)$_3$

Cobalt(II) nitrite

S	Co	NO$_2$
V	2	1
S	1	2
D	1	2
F		Co(NO$_2$)$_2$

Vanadium(IV) hydrogensulfate

S	V	HSO$_4$
V	4	1
S	1	4
D	1	4
F		V(HSO$_4$)$_4$

Zinc(II) phosphate

S	Zn	PO$_4$
V	2	3
S	3	2
D	3	2
F		Zn$_3$(PO$_4$)$_2$

Ruthenium(III) nitrate

S	Ru	NO$_3$
V	3	1
S	1	3
D	1	3
F		Ru(NO$_3$)$_3$

Palladium(II) sulfate

S	Pd	SO$_4$
V	2	2
S	2	2
D	1	1
F		PdSO$_4$

Copper(II) carbonate

S	Cu	CO$_3$
V	2	2
S	2	2
D	1	1
F		CuCO$_3$

Tungsten(III) cyanide

S   W   CN

V   3   1

S   1   3

D   1   3

F   W(CN)$_3$

Chromium(II) hypochlorite

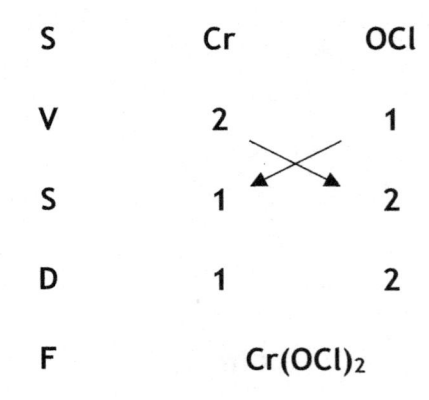

S   Cr   OCl

V   2   1

S   1   2

D   1   2

F   Cr(OCl)$_2$

Nickel(II) carbonate

S   Ni   CO$_3$

V   2   2

S   2   2

D   1   1

F   NiCO$_3$

Iron(III) phosphate

S   Fe   PO$_4$

V   3   3

S   3   3

D   1   1

F   FePO$_4$

Cadmium(II) hydroxide

S   Cd   OH

V   2   1

S   1   2

D   1   2

F   Cd(OH)$_2$

Niobium(V) nitrate

S   Nb   NO$_3$

V   5   1

S   1   5

D   1   5

F   Nb(NO$_3$)$_5$

Manganese(II) carbonate

S	Mn	CO₃
V	2	2
S	2	2
D	1	1
F	MnCO₃	

Silver(I) nitrate

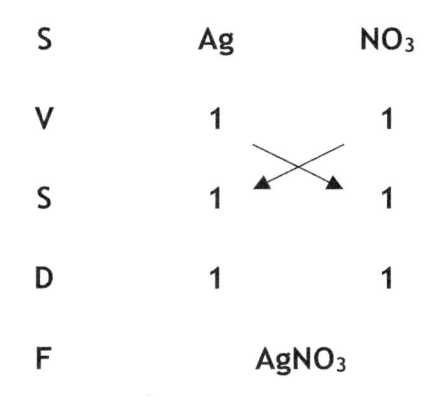

S	Ag	NO₃
V	1	1
S	1	1
D	1	1
F	AgNO₃	

Cobalt(II) hydroxide

S	Co	OH
V	2	1
S	1	2
D	1	2
F	Co(OH)₂	

Copper(I) chromate

S	Cu	CrO₄
V	1	1
S	1	1
D	1	1
F	CuCrO₄	

Zinc(II) sulfate

S	Zn	SO₄
V	2	2
S	2	2
D	1	1
F	ZnSO₄	

Nickel(II) phosphate

S	Ni	PO₄
V	2	3
S	3	2
D	3	2
F	Ni₃(PO₄)₂	

Exercise 7 — Answers

Sodium fluoride

S	Na$^+$	F$^-$
V	1	1
S	1	1
D	1	1
F	Na$^+$ F$^-$	

Magnesium oxide

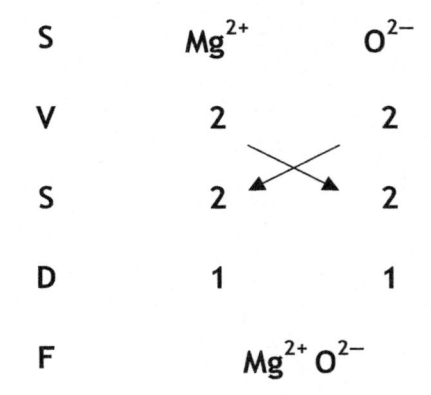

S	Mg^{2+}	O^{2-}
V	2	2
S	2	2
D	1	1
F	Mg^{2+} O^{2-}	

Lithium sulfide

S	Li$^+$	S^{2-}
V	1	2
S	2	1
D	2	1
F	(Li$^+$)$_2$ S^{2-}	

Copper(II) chloride

S	Cu^{2+}	Cl$^-$
V	2	1
S	1	2
D	1	2
F	Cu^{2+}(Cl$^-$)$_2$	

Aluminium oxide

S	Al^{3+}	O^{2-}
V	3	2
S	2	3
D	2	3
F	(Al^{3+})$_2$ (O^{2-})$_3$	

Potassium nitrate

S	K$^+$	NO$_3^-$
V	1	1
S	1	1
D	1	1
F	K$^+$NO$_3^-$	

Ammonium iodide

S	NH$_4^+$	I$^-$
V	1	1
S	1	1
D	1	1
F	NH$_4^+$I$^-$	

Vanadium(V) oxide

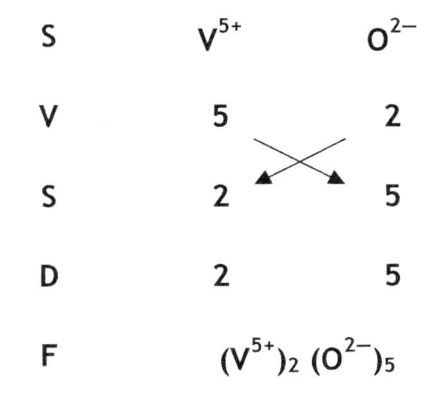

S	V^{5+}	O^{2-}
V	5	2
S	2	5
D	2	5
F	(V^{5+})$_2$ (O^{2-})$_5$	

Nickel(II) nitrate

S	Ni^{2+}	NO$_3^-$
V	2	1
S	1	2
D	1	2
F	Ni^{2+} (NO$_3^-$)$_2$	

Zinc(II) sulfite

S	Zn^{2+}	SO$_3^{2-}$
V	2	2
S	2	2
D	1	1
F	Zn^{2+}SO$_3^{2-}$	

Potassium hydrogencarbonate

S	K$^+$	HCO$_3^-$
V	1	1
S	1	1
D	1	1
F	K$^+$HCO$_3^-$	

Lithium nitride

S	Li$^+$	N^{3-}
V	1	3
S	3	1
D	3	1
F	(Li$^+$)$_3$ N^{3-}	

Calcium hydroxide

S	Ca^{2+}	OH$^-$
V	2	1
S	1	2
D	1	2
F	Ca^{2+}(OH$^-$)$_2$	

Cobalt(III) phosphate

S	Co^{3+}	PO$_4^{3-}$
V	3	3
S	3	3
D	1	1
F	Co^{3+}PO$_4^{3-}$	

Manganese(II) chloride

S	Mn^{2+}	Cl$^-$
V	2	1
S	1	2
D	1	2
F	Mn^{2+}(Cl$^-$)$_2$	

Copper(II) sulfate

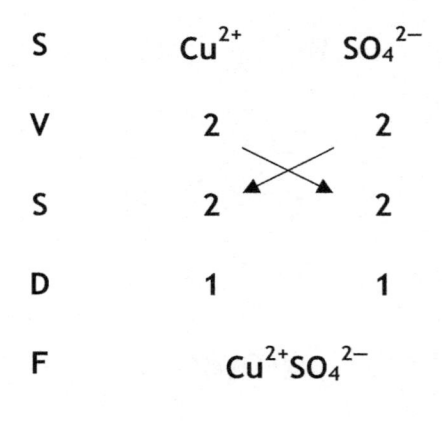

S	Cu^{2+}	SO$_4^{2-}$
V	2	2
S	2	2
D	1	1
F	Cu^{2+}SO$_4^{2-}$	

Rubidium iodide

S	Rb$^+$	I$^-$
V	1	1
S	1	1
D	1	1
F	Rb$^+$I$^-$	

Strontium nitrite

S	Sr^{2+}	NO$_2^-$
V	2	1
S	1	2
D	1	2
F	Sr^{2+}(NO$_2^-$)$_2$	

Ammonium cyanide			Chromium(IV) oxide		
S	NH₄⁺	CN⁻	S	Cr⁴⁺	O²⁻
V	1	1	V	4	2
S	1	1	S	2	4
D	1	1	D	1	2
F	NH₄⁺CN⁻		F	Cr⁴⁺(O²⁻)₂	

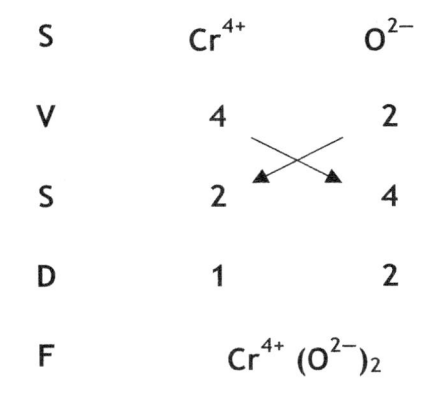

Sodium hypochlorite			Silver(I) sulfide		
S	Na⁺	ClO⁻	S	Ag⁺	S²⁻
V	1	1	V	1	2
S	1	1	S	2	1
D	1	1	D	2	1
F	Na⁺ClO⁻		F	(Ag⁺)₂ S²⁻	

Barium nitrate			Potassium permanganate		
S	Ba²⁺	NO₃⁻	S	K⁺	MnO₄⁻
V	2	1	V	1	1
S	1	2	S	1	1
D	1	2	D	1	1
F	Ba²⁺(NO₃⁻)₂		F	K⁺MnO₄⁻	

Printed in Great Britain
by Amazon